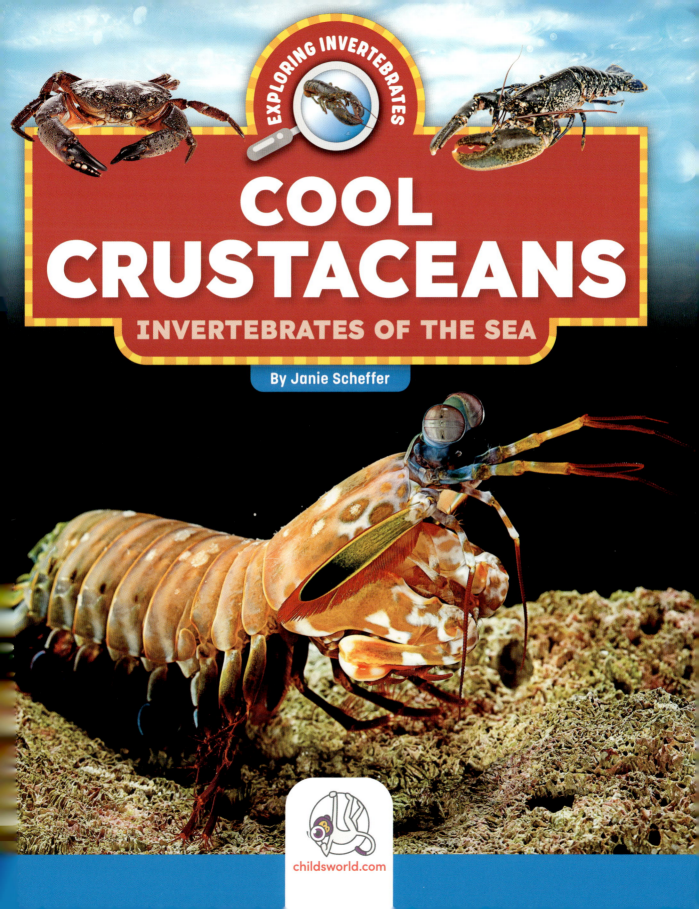

Published by The Child's World®
800-599-READ • childsworld.com

Copyright © 2025 by The Child's World®
All rights reserved. No part of this book may be reproduced or utilized in any form or by any means without written permission from the publisher.

Photography Credits
Cover: ©Africa Studio/Shutterstock; ©Zeeking/Shutterstock; ©Meena Meese/Shutterstock; PickPik/PickPik; Paul Starosta/Stone/Getting Images; pages4–5: ©Alessandro Rota/Getty Images/Shutterstock; page 5: ©Glenn Price/Shutterstock; page 5: ©prapat1120/Shutterstock; page 5: ©Zeeking/Shutterstock; page 6: ©Erik Isselee/Shutterstock; page 7: ©Global_Pics/iStock/Getty Images; page 7: ©1000s_pixels/Shutterstock; page 7: ©milan chanthorn/Shutterstock; page 7: ©EreborMountain/Shutterstock; page 8: ©Zeeking/Shutterstock; page 9: ©R A Kearton/Moment Open/Getty Images; page 10–11: ©Pavel Tochinsky/Photodisk/Getty Images; page 11: ©Ken Usami/Photodisk/Getty Images; page 12: ©Paul Starosta/Stone/Shutterstock; page 12: ©Brent Durand/Moment/Getty Images; page 13: ©Erik Isselee/Getty Images: page 14: ©Lotus Images/Shutterstock; page 15: ©Robert Pickett/Corbis Documentary/Getty Images; pages 16–17: ©FOTO JOURNEY/Shutterstock; page 17: ©b44022101/iStock/Getty Images; pages 18–19: ©symbiot/Shutterstock; page 20: ©Romolo Tavani/Shutterstock; page 20: ©YinYang/E+/Getty Images; page 22: ©Lori Bye; page 23: ©Eric Isselee/Shutterstock

ISBN Information
9781503894495 (Reinforced Library Binding)
9781503894761 (Portable Document Format)
9781503895584 (Online Multi-user eBook)
9781503896406 (Electronic Publication)

LCCN
2024942889

Printed in the United States of America

ABOUT THE AUTHOR

Janie Scheffer is an author and ELA curriculum writer. She has written more than 14 children's books about animals, sports, and social-emotional topics. She lives in Minnesota with her husband, daughter, and identical twin boys.

CONTENTS

CHAPTER 1
MEET SOME COOL CRUSTACEANS . . . 4

CHAPTER 2
CRABS AND SHRIMP . . . 10

CHAPTER 3
LIFE CYCLE OF A CRUSTACEAN . . . 14

CHAPTER 4
CRUSTACEANS IN THE WORLD . . . 18

CHAPTER 5
THE FUTURE OF CRUSTACEANS . . . 20

Wonder More . . . 21
Make a Crab! . . . 22
Glossary . . . 23
Find Out More . . . 24
Index . . . 24

CHAPTER 1

MEET SOME COOL CRUSTACEANS

A female American lobster crawls along the ocean floor. She carries 20,000 eggs with her. The eggs are stuck to small flippers on the bottom of her tail. She stops at a nesting spot. Her pincers flap and her claws drum. Is she dancing? No, she is communicating! This is how she lets nearby creatures know this is her spot.

This lobster is one of about 45,000 different **species** of crustaceans. The most known crustaceans are crabs, lobsters, shrimp, and woodlice. Crustaceans have been found in water and on land for about 540 million years!

SOME COMMON CRUSTACEANS

crab

shrimp

lobster

Shrimp usually travel in large groups known as schools. They can swim up to five miles (8.05 kilometers) per day.

Like spiders and insects, crustaceans are **arthropods**. Their legs are jointed. Most crustaceans have 10 legs, but they can have up to 14. Crustaceans are also invertebrates, which means they do not have a backbone. Their **exoskeletons** protect their bodies. Crustaceans **molt** many times before becoming adults!

Crustaceans come in many different sizes. The American lobster can weigh more than 40 pounds (18.1 kilograms). In comparison, the fairy shrimp weigh around 0.5 ounces (15 grams). No matter their size, crustaceans eat plants and algae, animals, and **plankton**.

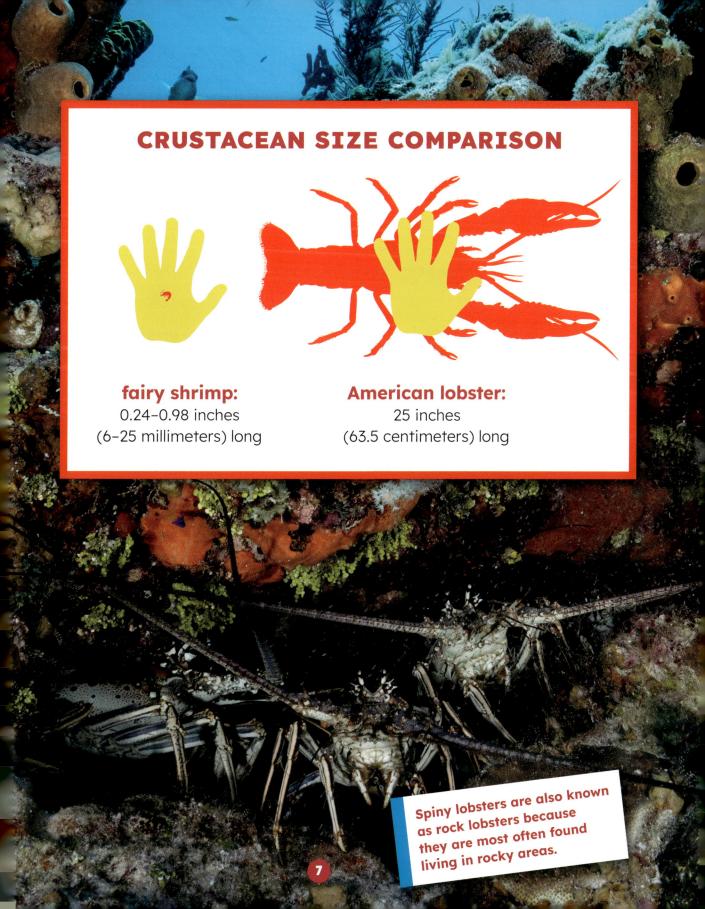

CRUSTACEAN SIZE COMPARISON

fairy shrimp:
0.24–0.98 inches
(6–25 millimeters) long

American lobster:
25 inches
(63.5 centimeters) long

Spiny lobsters are also known as rock lobsters because they are most often found living in rocky areas.

Crustaceans can be found all around the world. They live in a wide range of **habitats**. They are found mostly in fresh water and salt water. While some crustaceans are bottom dwellers, others live in shallow waters. On land, crustaceans live in rocky, muddy, and sandy places. Some even live on human-made things such as boats and docks!

Copepods are the easiest crustaceans to find. They have the biggest population of all crustaceans. They are a form of **zooplankton**. There are about 13,000 species of copepods. They can be found in both fresh and salt water.

WHERE IN THE WORLD DO CRUSTACEANS LIVE?:

Most lobsters can be found living on the ocean floor. Smaller lobsters hide within weeds and rocks. Bigger lobsters move to shallow waters in warmer seasons. In comparison, woodlice are most often found on land. They live under things such as rocks and compost piles. Barnacles can be found stuck to boats or buoys. Some even live attached to other barnacles!

There are more than 1,000 kinds of barnacles. They often live on walls and boats. But many even attach to other living things, including whales!

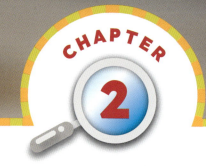

CHAPTER 2

CRABS AND SHRIMP

The giant Japanese spider crab has 10 long legs. Eight of their legs allow them to walk. Two of their legs, called **chelipeds**, have claws. This crustacean gets its name from its leg span. It measures 12.46 feet (3.8 meters) wide! If a giant Japanese spider crab loses a leg, it can grow a new one when it molts. Its exoskeleton protects its boneless body and can blend into the ocean floor. This is important because the giant Japanese spider crab does not swim—it walks. And it is a slow walker. Its shell provides **camouflage** to trick predators!

PARTS OF A CRAB

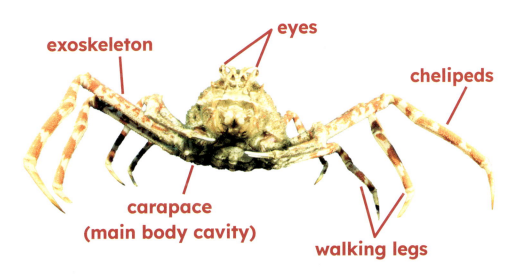

- exoskeleton
- eyes
- chelipeds
- carapace (main body cavity)
- walking legs

Ghost crabs are hard to see because they blend in with their surroundings. They spend most of the day underground and come out at night to hunt.

If a pistol shrimp's snapping claw is injured or damaged, its other claw grows larger to replace it.

Mantis shrimp have powerful eyes which allow them to see kinds of light that humans cannot.

MANTIS SHRIMP
There are more than 500 species of mantis shrimp. These crustaceans can be found in the shallow waters of the Indian and Pacific Oceans. They are known for their hunting strength. Some species spear their food using a spike on their leg. Others punch and smash their meal with a hammer-like claw. The speed of the punch is up to 50 miles (80 km) per hour.

The pistol shrimp is also called the snapping shrimp. It has a mighty talent. This crustacean is known for its fast claws. Some researchers have said the pistol shrimp has the fastest claws underwater, moving at 60.3 miles (97 kilometers) per hour! The speed of their claws is their defense mechanism. When they snap their claws, an air bubble is formed. This is not just any air bubble. It packs some power! When the air bubble pops it creates a shock wave, a flash of light, and a loud noise. Predators scatter at the sight and sound of this air bubble.

CHAPTER 3

LIFE CYCLE OF A CRUSTACEAN

Female crustaceans produce eggs. The number of eggs depends on the species. For example, crabs and lobsters produce up to 100,000 eggs. Shrimp can produce up to 1 million eggs, and woodlice up to 150 eggs. After the egg stage, crustaceans become **larvae**. In the larval and juvenile stages, crustaceans molt more than once to grow into their adult bodies. Freshwater crabs and crayfish hatch from their eggs already looking like adults!

Although they look similar to spiders, arrow crabs are crustaceans that live in the ocean. They often avoid being attacked by attaching objects to their bodies to make themselves less appealing.

Most crustaceans live freely, roaming on land and swimming in the water. But some crustaceans are **parasitic**. This means they live attached to a host and feed on its body. Fish lice, sea lice, and whale lice are some examples of parasitic crustaceans. Barnacles also do not move freely. They stick themselves to ships, boats, buoys, docks, other sea life—and even other barnacles. They do not feed off their hosts. Instead, they eat plankton floating in the water.

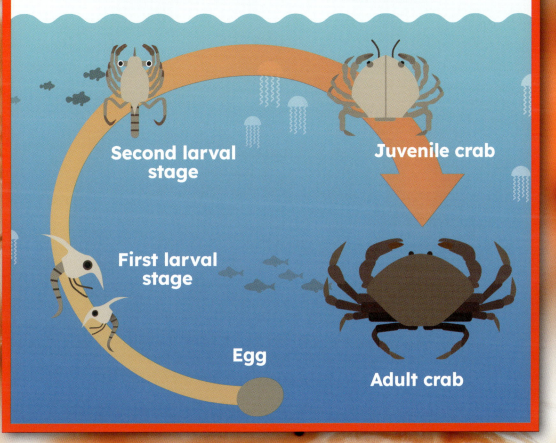

Brine shrimp are only about 0.4 inches (one centimeter) long. They are a major food source for water birds such as flamingoes.

CHAPTER 4

CRUSTACEANS IN THE WORLD

Crustaceans play an important role in the marine **ecosystem**. When small crustaceans eat algae, plants are healthier and the water is cleaner. They help keep oceans clean and healthy. A reef is healthier when many species of crustaceans live on or near it. Some crustaceans are **filter feeders** that improve the water quality by recycling nutrients. On land, crustaceans keep the ground clean by eating dead animals and plants. In addition, crustaceans are important food for larger marine creatures such as fish and whales.

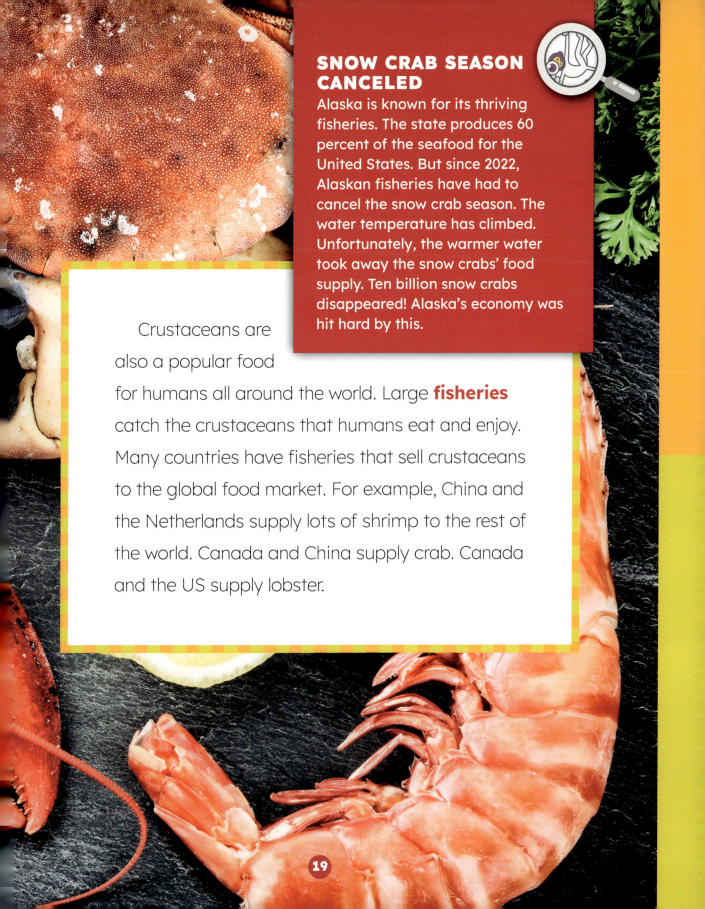

SNOW CRAB SEASON CANCELED

Alaska is known for its thriving fisheries. The state produces 60 percent of the seafood for the United States. But since 2022, Alaskan fisheries have had to cancel the snow crab season. The water temperature has climbed. Unfortunately, the warmer water took away the snow crabs' food supply. Ten billion snow crabs disappeared! Alaska's economy was hit hard by this.

Crustaceans are also a popular food for humans all around the world. Large **fisheries** catch the crustaceans that humans eat and enjoy. Many countries have fisheries that sell crustaceans to the global food market. For example, China and the Netherlands supply lots of shrimp to the rest of the world. Canada and China supply crab. Canada and the US supply lobster.

CHAPTER 5
THE FUTURE OF CRUSTACEANS

Crustaceans are not just cool creatures. They're also important to our world! They clean the waters they live in, and they clean the land they live on. Without crustaceans, the environment would not be as healthy. Crustaceans are food for larger animals. They are food for humans, too. The global crustacean food market is growing because of the need. In general, people are wanting to eat more crustaceans! As some of the oldest animals on Earth, crustaceans are key to both the ecosystem and economy.

WONDER MORE

Wondering About New Information

What is one new fact you learned about crustaceans? Why did this fact stick out to you? Explain.

Wondering How It Matters

Crustaceans are important food for other animals and for humans. Crustaceans create many jobs in the food industry. How can humans respect the crustacean population? Why is it important for humans to be respectful of these animals?

Wondering Why

Why do you think crustaceans are an important part of the marine ecosystem? What are some of the things they do to improve water and land?

Ways to Keep Wondering

After reading this book, what questions do you still have about crustaceans? Which crustacean would you like to know more about?

MAKE A CRAB!

Steps to Take

1. Paint one hand with red paint. Press your hand down on the white paper.

2. Paint your other hand with red paint. Press your hand down on the white paper, overlapping your handprints by just a bit at the palms.

3. Cut out two white circles for the eyes. Use black paint to paint the inside of each eye. Glue the eyes onto your crab (on the thumbs).

4. Use black paint to add a smile in the middle of the crab's face.

Supplies
- white paper
- red paint
- black paint
- paintbrushes
- scissors
- glue

GLOSSARY

arthropods (AR-thruh-pods) Arthropods are a large group of animals with hard shells, jointed legs, and no bones.

camouflage (KAM-uh-flazh) Camouflage is a disguise that helps an animal blend into its surroundings.

chelipeds (KEE-luh-peds) Chelipeds are the two legs of a decapod that have claws.

ecosystem (EE-koh-sis-tum) An ecosystem is a group of creatures and environments that work together.

exoskeletons (eks-oh-SKEL-uh-tunz) Exoskeletons are hard outer shells.

filter feeders (FIL-ter FEE-ders) Filter feeders are animals that get their food by filtering food from the water.

fisheries (FISH-uh-rees) Fisheries are businesses that catch and sell fish and seafood.

habitat (HAB-uh-tat) A habitat is where an animal lives.

larvae (LAHR-vee) Larvae are animals after they hatch from eggs and before they become adults.

molt (MOHLT) Molt means to shed skin, feathers, fur, or horns and grow a new outer covering.

parasitic (par-uh-SIT-ik) Parasitic is when an organism takes nutrients from another organism.

plankton (PLANK-ton) Plankton are very small plants and animals floating in fresh water and salt water.

species (SPEE-sheez) A species is a group of living things that are able to reproduce.

zooplankton (zo-uh-PLAYNK-ton) Zooplankton are very small plankton or the eggs and larvae of fish and other sea creatures.

FIND OUT MORE

In the Library

Brundle, Joanna. *Crustaceans*. New York, NY: KidHaven Publishing, 2020.

Cocca, Lisa Colozza. *Arthropods*. North Mankato, MN: Rourke Educational Media, 2019.

Pallotta, Jerry. *The Crab Alphabet Book*. Watertown, MA: Charlesbridge, 2019.

On the Web

Visit our website for links about crustaceans:
childsworld.com/links

Note to Parents, Caregivers, Teachers, and Librarians: We routinely verify our web links to make sure they are safe and active sites. So encourage your readers to check them out!

INDEX

barnacles, 9, 16

claws, 4, 10, 12–13
crabs, 4, 10–11, 14–15, 19

eggs, 4, 14, 17

food, 13, 17–21

habitat, 8

legs, 6, 10–11
lobsters, 4, 7, 9, 14

mantis shrimp, 13

pincers, 4